Wellingborough

on old picture

Clive Guest and Andrew Swift

Market Hill, Wellingboro.

1. The Corn Exchange was built in 1861 and pulled down, just short of its century, in 1959. By the time this card was published in 1914, it had become the 'Electric Theatre,' where short films were interspersed with variety acts. It later became the Regal Cinema. This card was published in the 'PN' series of 'Artistic Cards.'

£3.50

INTRODUCTION

It is generally reckoned that Wellingborough was founded by a Saxon leader called Waendel. Spelling was not, however, one of the stronger points of our distant ancestors and for about 600 years the name of the town alternated between variants of Waendelburg and Welingburgh.

It was the growing fame of the waters of the Red Well which finally clinched the issue in favour of "Welingburgh". By the early years of the 17th century, it looked as though the town might develop into a fashionable spa. When King Charles I and Queen Henrietta decided to spend nine days in the town to take the waters, it only seemed a matter of time before the fashionable world would beat a path to its door. Unfortunately, the small matter of a Civil War intervened. Charles's death on the scaffold in 1649 effectively put paid to the town's dreams of glory.

In the centuries which followed, Wellingborough slowly developed as a market town and manufacturing centre, specialising in lace and leather. By the middle of the 19th century, lace-making was on the decline, but the arrival of the railway in 1845 paved the way for a new industry, iron making, which drew on the rich deposits of ironstone in and around the town.

At the beginning of the 19th century, Wellingborough had a population of 3,325. In the next 50 years, it grew steadily and reached 5,061 by 1851. In the second half of the 19th century, however, the population exploded. By 1901 it stood at 19,753 - almost four times what it had been 50 years earlier.

The postcards in this book, most of which date from the first quarter of the 20th century, show the effects of this rapid expansion. Older buildings such as the 'Hind Hotel' and the 'Golden Lion' in Sheep Street, and the old Grammar School in the churchyard are outnumbered by buildings which must have appeared very new at the time. The late-lamented Corn Exchange, for example, was only 39 years old at the beginning of the 20th century - only as old as a building put up in 1960 is for us today.

So, while the postcards we've chosen may seem to reflect a lost golden age, for the people who appear on them Wellingborough must have felt a decidedly modern town. And it was changing all the time. Take Midland Road, for example. Our first view of it dates from around 1905. The second, from only three years later, shows big changes - the 'Old King's Arms' has appeared at the top of the street and the final touches are being put to the new Post Office. In the next view, dating from 1936, it's all change again, as the 'Lyric' cinema and petrol station have sprung up across the road.

Bigger changes still were to follow. An agreement signed in 1962 between the town council and the Greater London Council was the signal for a massive expansion programme which has seen much of the "old" town swept away in its wake. Today one side of Midland Road is dominated by the Swansgate Centre. The 'Lyric', the Post Office and much else has disappeared.

Wellingborough has seen many changes in the 20th century, yet the pace of change is quickening all the time. It's interesting to speculate how far we will get into the 21st century before the Wellingborough we know today will seem as remote as some of the scenes which follow.

Clive Guest & Andrew Swift
April 1999

Front cover: The half-timbered building in Market Street, dating from 1907, once housed Boot's Chemists, Noble & Billingham's, and the Cosy Cafe. On the right is Smith's Chemists. This view was published by J. Lees of Northampton, and posted from Wellingborough in October 1908.

The River & Promenade, Wellingborough.

2. The embankment was built in 1931. In this view, dating from around 1933, a goods train can be seen on the bridge linking Wellingborough's two stations.

The Walk, Wellingborough

3. A view of the Walks, with the cricket field on the left. Shortly after the Walks were planted in the early 19th century, a large number of the saplings were vandalised, which prompted a Mr Wilkin to publish a pamphlet attacking *"that Goth - that double-distilled vandal - that brutal iconoclast, who dared to destroy those trees which imaged forth as it were, the good intention of the planters, those trees which would have been the pride and comfort of the future sons of Wellingborough - under whose shade the tales of lovers yet unborn would have been told. I say again, accursed be the destroyer!"* And so on. They don't write them like that any more! Card published by Valentine of Dundee in their 'XL' series.

4. Wellingborough's first station, on the Blisworth-Peterborough branch of the London & Birmingham Railway, opened on 2nd June 1845. As the caption on this card published by J. Horden & Sons of Wellingborough indicates, the station was actually in Little Irchester. When the Midland Railway opened its main line through Wellingborough on 8th May 1857, it took much of the traffic away from the old route. Wellingborough London Road closed to passengers on 4th May 1964, although goods trains used the old station until the early 1980's. Today all traces of the station have disappeared and the A45 flyover dominates this scene.

WB 32   WELLINGBOROUGH COUNTY HIGH SCHOOL   A TUCK CARD

5. The Girls' High School, now the Wrenn School, opened in 1911. It is seen here from the London Road on a postcard published by the leading card firm Raphael Tuck & Sons.

V377-7

WELLINGBOROUGH. GIRL'S GRAMMAR SCHOOL.

RAPID PHOTO. E.C

6. The original Girls' High was on Midland Road. Founded in 1907, it closed in 1911 when the building on London Road opened. This house later became the Lindens residential home. The card was published by the Rapid Photo Printing Co., and posted in March 1912: *"Just a postcard to let you know I have not forgot you, glad to hear you got the hair nets home safe."*

The Grammar School. Wellingborough.

7. Wellingborough Grammar School moved to London Road in 1881. It previously occupied the building on the north side of the churchyard.

8. A card from Horden showing the new cattle market shortly after opening in 1905. Prior to this, the cattle market was held at the top end of the Market Place. Part of the building in the background has now been incorporated into the Castle Theatre. The message on the postcard, sent on 30th November 1905, went: *"Thanks so much for the postcard this morning. Have sent you one of the New Market."*

9. In the 1920's it was the custom for the Chairman of the Council to plant a tree in Doddington Road to mark his year in office. Here Councillor Peck, chairman in 1923, looks on while his wife wields the spade. The Pecks' eldest daughter is on the left. Published by A.T. Watts, Central Studio, Silver Street, Wellingborough.

V377-8   WELLINGBOROUGH COTTAGE HOSPITAL AND DODDINGTON ROAD   RAPID PHOTO E C

10. Doddington Road Hospital opened in 1900 with seventeen beds. In this view from just before the First World War, it could be in the middle of the country. Another card by the London firm Rapid Photo, posted in August 1913.

11. A view of Swanspool around 1905. This late 18th century building, together with its extensive grounds, was given to the town in 1918 by Mr F.C. Chamberlain. An anonymously-published card, postally used in August 1928.

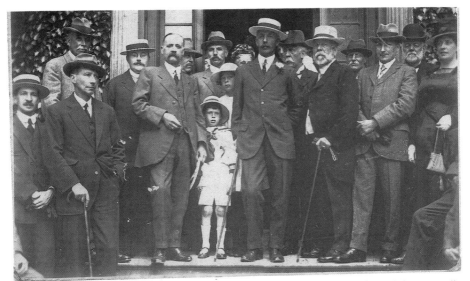

12. A group of councillors standing outside Swanspool at the opening of the council offices on June 15th 1919. Left to right: O.W. Davis (Councillor), C. Parker (Deputy Clerk to the Council), J. B. Whitworth (Councillor & County Councillor), John Peck (Chairman of the Pleasure Grounds Committe), J.(?) Edwards (Chairman of the Council), R. Gregson (Councillor), Walter Chamberlain (Councillor), F.C. Chamberlain (Donor of Swanspool) with his two children, Sir Ryland Adkins, K.C (Chairman of the County Council), George Benson (Councillor), J.A. Gotch (Kettering), John Lea (Vice Chairman of the Council), Tom Sanders (Councillor), Mrs George Hacksley (Councillor). Mrs Wakeham and Mrs F.C. Chamberlain are at the back.

13. The bowling green and Swanspool Pavilion in 1938, a scene virtually unchanged today.The card was posted in August 1938. No. 13 in a series of cards by unknown publisher.

14. The bottom of Sheep Street around 1905. The 'Golden Lion,' which dates from the mid 16th century, is on the right. The two buildings above it are still standing, but those further along, which included Gladys Moon's sweet shop and Lack's florists, were demolished when Commercial Way was built. Until well into the 19th century an annual sheep fair was held in Sheep Street on St Lukes' Day (29th October), with as many as 10,000 sheep changing hands. Published by Photochrom, and posted at Swansea in September 1908.

15. A group of Wellingborough schoolboys stand outside the old houses on Sheep Street. The small gable second from the right was removed when the houses were restored in the 1920's. Next door to the houses were Praed's clock office and the 'Bee's Wing' pub. Both have now been demolished, although the clock has found a new home in Burystead Place. This card was sent from Wellingborough on Christmas Eve 1906.

WB 7 · THE ZOO PARK, WELLINGBOROUGH · A TUCK CARD

16. Wellingborough Zoo Park around 1950. The entrance to this was to the left of the old houses in Sheep Street. After the closure of the zoo around 1970, Croyland Abbey, in the background, fell derelict and was threatened with demolition. It was saved by the council, who used it to house their planning department. Apart from the Abbey, this scene is virtually unrecognisable today as a large council office block dominates the scene. Card published by Raphael Tuck, and postally used in 1950.

17. Looking down Sheep Street shortly before the First World War. On the corner is Burnett's hatters, with Green and Valentine's drapers on the left. Below Burnett's is Horden's toy shop, which published this card. It was posted in July 1917: *"Amy and I have just walked into Wollaston, and I am writing this in uncle's trap whilst holding the horse for him."*

18. The Market Place around 1905, with the 17th century 'Hind Hotel' and the 'Crown Inn' (on the far left). The drinking fountain and horse trough were presented to the town in 1903 by James Page. Card published by Stewart & Woolf, posted at Wellingborough in July 1905.

19. A Raphael Tuck postcard of Market Street in the late 1940's, showing the 'Old King's Arms' and the Granville Hotel and Cafe, built in 1882 as a temperance hotel. Published by Raphael Tuck.

20. A 1930's view of Market Street. On the far side of Pebble Lane are the old Barclays Bank building and the original Woolworths.

21. Noble's grocery shop in Market Street - an advertising card posted at Wellingborough in June 1911. Today the Nationwide Anglia Building Society occupies this building.

NOBLE'S GROCERY STORES.

THE ARCADE,
14, MARKET STREET,
WELLINGBOROUGH

Market Square, Wellingborough.

22. A view of the Market Square in 1913, the year Wellingborough got its first bus service - a circular route linking Rushden, Higham Ferrers, Irthlingborough and Finedon. Buses were ultramarine blue with red upper-deck panels, waistband and wheels and white window surrounds. All the buildings in this picture have since been demolished. Card published by Horden.

WELLINGBORO' MARKET, WEDNESDAY, MAY 26TH, 1920.
MESSRS. GILLITT & GILLITT, AUCTIONEERS.

23. Gillitt and Gillitt held regular auctions outside their offices in the market place. In this 1920 view, three sales are underway - shoes nearest the camera, chickens in the middle distance and carts by the churchyard wall. The Corn Exchange is on the right. Card published by A.T. Watts, and posted at Wellingborough in February 1931.

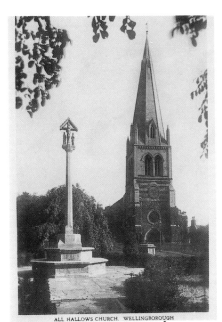

24. A view of the Market Square in the 1950's. There has been a regular market at Wellingborough since 1200, and, until 1905, this was the site of the cattle market. Raphael Tuck postcard, posted at Cambridge in October 1955.

25. The Parish Church of All Hallows was known as St Luke's in the early 20th century. In this view from the 1920's, published by Horden, the church war memorial can be seen on the left.

26. An early view of the old grammar school from the churchyard. This building housed the grammar school from 1595 to 1881, when the school on London Road opened. The building is now used as a church hall. *"Are you still in the land of the living? Should be pleased if you will be kind enough to reciprocate as I am collecting. I have several hundred already,"* wrote the sender.

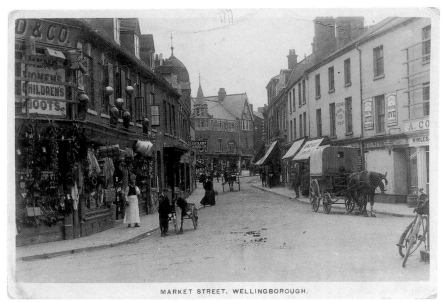

MARKET STREET, WELLINGBOROUGH.

27. Market Street around 1910. On the left is Ward's pawnbrokers. Shops on the right include Simco's chemists, Vorley's outfitters and the Geisha Tea-room. Card published by C.F.P., Northampton.

28. Gloucester Place with the' Palace Cinema,' dating from 1911, on the left. This replaced the 'Empire Music Hall' which burnt down in 1909. On the opposite corner is Brown's tobacconist and hairdressers, with Dexter's ironmongers next door. Gloucester Place was originally called Hog Hill. Its change of name apparently came about as a result of the Duke of Gloucester's coach overturning as it rounded the corner from Church Street in the 1830's.

29. Brown's tobacconists and newsagents on an advertising card from around 1910. Upstairs, false teeth could be obtained from Mr W.H. Peck. Hootton's bazaar was on the right. Postcard published by Photochrom.

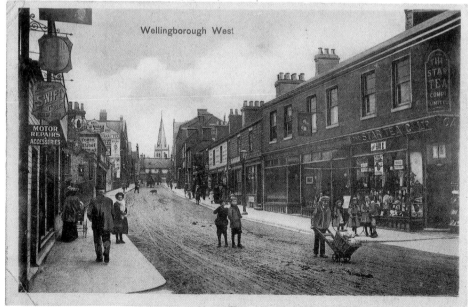

30. A view of Midland Road around 1905, before the Post Office and the 'Old King's Arms' were built. The 'Lyric Cinema' and petrol station were later built on the left. The postcard was published by Stewart & Woolf, and posted to Lincoln in August 1905: *"All being well we shall hope to arrive in Lincoln about 7.30 p.m."*

V377-5 WELLINGBOROUGH POST OFFICE. MIDLAND ROAD RAPID PHOTO. C C

31. Midland Road Post Office was still not complete when this photograph was taken in 1908. Just below it is the Midland Hotel. The 'Old King's Arms' is at the top of the street on this card published by the Rapid Photo Printing Co., posted at Wellingborough in August 1908.

22875. Midland Road, Wellingborough.

32. A view of the eagle house on Midland Road around the time of the First World War. Wilford's Auctioneers now occupies premises on the left. Card published by Horden and posted at Wellingborough in June 1919.

33. A view of the 'Lyric Cinema' and petrol station shortly after they opened in 1936. 'The Lyric' was pulled down in 1974 to make way for the Arndale Centre.

Midland Rd, Wellingborough.

34. Castle Fields in the early 1920's from the bottom of Brook Street. In the background is the Union Workhouse, which later became a hospital and is now being converted into flats. The saplings which can just be seen flanking the path in the middle of the picture are now part of the avenue of large trees which crosses the park. Card published by Horden and posted at Wellingborough in August 1924.

35. An early view of Castle Road with the cattle market on the right. Published by Express Photo Co., Rugby.

36. All Saints' School in Castle Street was built in 1881 for 398 children. This school photo dates from 1906.

37. The 'Volunteer' public house on Midland Road. Henry Rixon was the landlord in the early 1920's. He was also Drum Major of the Wellingborough Rifle Volunteer Band and is seen here in his uniform.

H. E. RIXON . . . . . Proprietor.

38. Silver Street around 1905 on a card by Valentine, with Serjeant's chemists and Wharton's Central Library on the left, and Freeman, Hardy & Willis's on the right.

39. The top of Silver Street on a postcard sent in October 1905, with the Angel Hotel, an old coaching inn, on the left. This was the site of an annual horse fair which continued until well into the 19th century.

40. A view looking up Silver Street in the late 1920's. The YMCA was built around 1900 as the Liberal Club. Card published by Photochrom,and posted at Rushden in August 1927.

SILVER STREET WELLINGBOROUGH.

S 2364

41. Silver Street around 1913 with Redhead's confectioners and Freeman, Hardy and Willis's on the left and Wharton's on the right. Published by W.H. Smith in their 'Kingsway' series, and posted at Northampton in June 1913.

42. Cambridge Street on a Horden postcard from around 1910. Shops include Allured's tobacconists, Warne's tailors and Maycock's Stores. The 'Crispin Arms' - named after St Crispin, patron saint of shoemakers - is on the left.

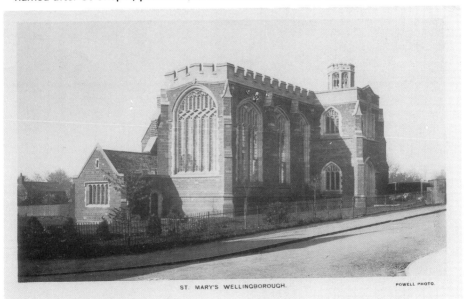

ST. MARY'S WELLINGBOROUGH.   POWELL PHOTO

43. The parish of St Mary's was formed from the parish of All Saints in 1904. Here the church is seen before the tower and a large part of the building were added. The architect was Sir Ninian Comper and the stone used came from Finedon and Weldon. Card published by Powell.

44. All Saints on Midland Road was consecrated in 1868. The vicarage on the right has since been demolished and the new police station occupies the site.

45. The Baptist Church in Mill Road was built in 1905. The spire was removed after it became unsafe.

46. Mill Road around 1910, looking east from outside the Masonic Hall. The houses on the right are much the same today. Betty's Pantry can be seen on the far corner of Strode Road, with the spire of the Baptist Church in the distance.

47. Looking up Stanley Road around 1910. This street probably dates from around 1892, as houses on the right (not shown in this view) bear this date. Cooke's mineral water plant can be seen on the far corner of Grant Road.

VICTORIA SCHOOL, WELLINGBOROUGH

48. Victoria Board School (now the Junior School) celebrated its centenary in 1995. This viewcard was posted from the town in July 1905.

St. Barnabas Church, Wellingborough.

49. St Barnabas Church was built in 1893 as a Chapel of Ease to replace a temporary building which had been in use since the 1860's. It was destroyed by fire in 1949. The present building dates from 1954. Postcard published by W.A. Nichols, Wellingborough.

50. Lilliman's bakery and Geary's general store can be seen in this view of College Street dating from around 1905. The front gable of the old St Barnabas Church can be seen above the houses on the right. Published by the Express Photo Co. of Rugby.

51. The Co-op Crimson Ramblers form part of a carnival procession at the corner of College Street and Westfield Road, probably in the 1920's. Money collected by the carnival went to support the cottage hospital. The allotments in the background are now the site of Cox's Boot and Shoe factory.

52. Class II of St Barnabas Infants School face the camera around 1908.

53. Bassett's Close in the 1920's. In the Second World War, US tanks were stored on stands around the bandstand. The Americans also used St. Barnabas Church Hall as a storeroom.

54. Park Road with the Tabernacle Baptist Church, dating from 1863, on the left and Gent's plumbers on the right. A Horden card, published about 1905.

55. In this view looking down Park Road, dating from around 1910, Gent's plumbers can just be seen behind the tree in the foreground. The view is virtually unchanged today.

Council Chamber and Technical Institute, Wellingborough.

56. The old Technical College in Church Street also housed the Council Chamber before it moved to Swanspool in 1919. This building was pulled down in 1968 to make way for the car park for the new Technical College. Another Horden postcard, posted at Wellingborough in June 1909.

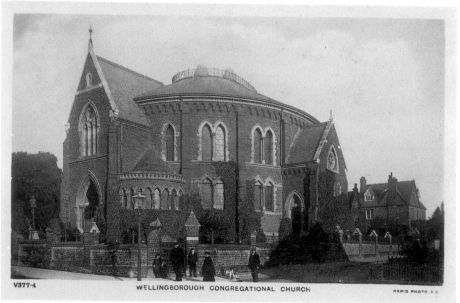

V377-4   WELLINGBOROUGH CONGREGATIONAL CHURCH   RAPID PHOTO. & C

57. The Congregational Chapel in the High Street was built in 1875 at a cost of £12,000. In this view dating from around 1910, the old manse can be seen in the background. The Job Centre now occupies the site of the manse. Published by Rapid Photo Printing Co.

58. A children's parade passing down High Street around 1910. A photo taken by Stanley Wones from his photographic studio. In the background is Edward's furniture store. In the early 20th century, "School Treat Days" were held once a year. All the children from Free Church Sunday Schools in the town would assemble on Broad Green and march through the town to Bassett's Close, where sporting events were held.

BROAD GREEN WITH HATTON HALL IN BACKGROUND, WELLINGBOROUGH

59. Looking up Broad Green before the War Memorial was built. Hatton Hall can just be glimpsed through the trees in the background. This card was postally used at Wellingborough in February 1917.

V377-6   WELLINGBOROUGH. BROAD GREEN   RAPID PHOTO E C

60. Looking down into Broad Green. Cattle markets and fairs were once held here and an ox-roast was held as late as 1897. Card published by the Rapid Photo Printing Co. and posted at Duffield in September 1910.

61. The War Memorial on Broad Green, dedicated on 11th November 1924. The names of 663 men and boys from Wellingborough who died in the First World War are recorded on the memorial. 126 more names were added after the Second World War.

62. Looking up Harrowden Road from Hatton Park Gardens. Salisbury House is behind the trees in the centre. A modern bungalow now occupies the site of the ironstone cottages on the left. As this is now the junction of the A509 and A510, it is unlikely that the girls on the card would appear quite so confident if they were standing in the same spot today. Card published by Horden, and posted c. 1913.

The Avenue, Gold St.

Wellingborough,

PHOTO. WATTS. WELLINGBOROUGH.

63. The cottage at the top of the Avenue in a view dating from around 1905. Still recognisable today, although the trees in the foreground have grown somewhat in the meantime. Card published by Watts.

64. A view of the Avenue Infants School dating from around 1912. Published by the London firm of Gottschalk, Dreyfus & Davis.

65. Wilby Road, showing Wilby Grange shortly after it was built for Edwin Parr in 1910. It was demolished in the 1960's and the site is now occupied by modern houses. Published by Rotary for J. Lees, Northampton.

WE/61   NORTHAMPTON ROAD. WELLINGBOROUGH

66. Northampton Road looking towards the town centre in the 1950's, with Weavers Road on the left. Harvey Road has since been built on the right. The houses along Northampton Road date from the inter-war years.

FINEDON ROAD, WELLINGBOROUGH.

67. Looking up Finedon Road around 1914 on another Horden postcard, postally used in February 1915. Chapman's box factory is on the left. Eastfield Park, which can be seen in the distance, was once an ironstone quarry.